Eighteenth-century

French porcelain

in the Ashmolean Museum

Aileen Dawson

CW00819511

Ashmolean Museum Oxford
1996

Published with the aid of a generous grant from the
Ceramica-Stiftung, Basel

Titles in this series include:
Drawings by Michelangelo and Raphael
Ruskin's drawings
Camille Pissarro and his family
Oxford and the Pre-Raphaelites
Worcester porcelain
Italian maiolica
Islamic ceramics
Indian paintings from Oxford collections

British Library Cataloguing in Publication Data
Dawson, Aileen
          Eighteenth-century French porcelain in the
          Ashmolean Museum (Ashmolean handbooks)
          I. Title II. Series
          738.20944
          ISBN 1 85444 075 6 (paperback)
          ISBN 1 85444 076 4 (hardback)

Cover illustration: Snuff-box, number 30

Designed by Cole design unit, Reading
Set in Versailles by Meridian Phototypesetting Limited
Printed and bound in Singapore by Toppan Printing Co.

Introduction

The Ashmolean Museum collection of French porcelain now consists of well over one hundred items. It has only come into existence since the end of the Second World War through the generosity of four benefactors: Sir Bernard Eckstein Bt., L.R. Abel Smith, Cyril A. de Costa Andrade and W.R.B. Young, and with the support of the Grant-in-Aid Fund administered by the Victoria and Albert Museum. The magnificent and important Sèvres biscuit (unglazed) porcelain figure of Pascal (50) was purchased for the collection through this Fund, aided by the National Art Collections Fund and two Museum funds. The growth of the collection is a sign of continuing interest in and appreciation of the porcelain made in France in the eighteenth century. The purpose of this book is to celebrate the range and strength of the collection, which is still growing. It is particularly remarkable not just for several pieces from famous collections, such as that of Count Xavier de Chavagnac (his sale was held in Paris in 1910 and pieces bearing his distinctive collection label can be found in all the major museum collections) but for the way it charts the development of porcelain in France from its beginnings in the late seventeenth-early eighteenth century and for the next eight decades. But the writer's aim has not solely been to trace this process. She has been particularly concerned to illustrate what she considers the most attractive, rare and important pieces in the collection, as well as some which were obviously part of routine production given the quantity that survive. For reasons of space some fine pieces (and some controversial ones) cannot be included here.

The first of the collectors, Sir Bernard Eckstein (1894–1948), attended Trinity College, Oxford. He became a wealthy businessman who built up a fine collection, consisting principally of Sèvres porcelains of the highest quality as well as some exciting Du Paquier (early to mid-eighteenth century Viennese) pieces, in the years after the First World War. Records in the British Museum show that several of his more splendid purchases were made through the Bond Street firm of Mallett. John Francis Mallett was himself one of the greatest benefactors of the Ashmolean. However, Eckstein seems to have had little interest in the past history of his pieces, which, in general, he liked to be rare or showy. In his will he bequeathed 187 pieces to the Ashmolean, including glass and coins.

Memories of the eccentric dealer F.V.C. de Costa Andrade (1882–1973), known as Cyril Andrade, live on, not least in Oxford, where his tendency to use the Museum as a store for pieces which he later sold was regarded with some coolness, despite his immense generosity to the Museum. In his last years he systematically helped build up the French porcelain collection (he presented other outstanding pieces such as the Chelsea porcelain head given in 1965 in memory of Sir Winston Churchill) in collaboration with the Museum staff. Andrade was a member of a Portuguese Jewish family. His great-grandfather settled in London, made a fortune from selling ostrich feathers, and acquired property in the City. Andrade himself, like his father before him, was an antique dealer based in the West Country (he gave a collection of Martinware and ceramics by Bernard Moore to Plymouth City Museum). His obituary in the *Daily Telegraph* (he died on 19 November 1973) states that he served twenty years on the Westminster City Council. His taste and knowledge were almost unrivalled, and the pieces he gave to the Ashmolean, many of which cost him considerable sums, ensured that it became one of the finest collections in England outside London.

Andrade's gift was made in 1968, the same year that Lionel Robert Abel Smith (1893–1968) bequeathed further French porcelains to the Museum. A scion of a banking family, an Etonian and an undergraduate at New College, Oxford, where he took a first in history in 1914, Abel Smith was almost blind by the time he became a Fellow of All Souls in 1919. Although he remained there until 1926, he spent much of his life as a virtual recluse. It is perhaps, therefore, surprising that he collected both Oriental and European porcelains, although the choice of a Meissen porcelain dish from the so-called 'Swan Service' with its extraordinary relief moulding is perhaps not so hard to understand. As well as his bequest, Mr Abel Smith made gifts in 1963 and 1967.

The last benefactor, William Richard Blackman Young (1895–1971), was a solicitor in the Hastings area. For several years at the end of his life he was a Brother of the Hospital of Saint Cross, Winchester, but retained his collection nevertheless. We have no knowledge of Young's background to explain his predilection for porcelain.

The diversity of the Ashmolean's collection, which is still growing, would be enough to ensure its position, for it contains some particularly rare and interesting pieces (see 10). However, it appeals not only to the scholar and specialist but also to the gallery visitor in search of visual delights. Many of the pieces from the factories operating in France before 1750 have a special charm which few can resist. I am greatly honoured to present them for the first time in book form for the greater enjoyment of all those who love porcelain.

Note on the factories
Eight different known factories are represented in this selection (Vincennes/Sèvres is counted as one). The origin of several pieces (9, 51 and 52) is at present uncertain. Only one (50) is of 'true' or 'hard-paste' porcelain, containing china clay, or kaolin, which was not in general use in France

until the early 1770s, shortly after china clay was discovered in the Limoges area. The remainder are of 'soft-paste' porcelain, essentially a glassy substance, which has the translucency but not the durability of true porcelain, but has been much prized by collectors. Space does not permit full factory histories. These may be found in the present writer's *Catalogue of French Porcelain in the British Museum* (1994). In brief, all the factories represented are in the environs of Paris. Saint-Cloud began in the early 1690s and closed down in 1766. Some small concerns operated in Paris in the second and third decades of the eighteenth century – their history is still being written. Chantilly was established around 1730 and granted a patent in 1735. Unlike the others, it used a tin glaze to give a whiter appearance to its porcelain. The factory continued into our own century, with many changes of ownership. The factory at Mennecy, which was in production from about 1750, was the direct successor of one at nearby Villeroy probably set up in 1737 and closed in 1748. Mennecy moved to Bourg-la-Reine in 1773. The Vincennes factory was founded in 1740, moved to Sèvres in 1756 and was purchased by the King in 1759. It alone survives today. Confusingly, another factory at Vincennes was operated by Sieur Seguin making hard-paste porcelain from 1774 to around 1788.

Acknowledgments
The author is deeply grateful to Mrs Dinah Reynolds, Voluntary Assistant in the Department of Western Art, without whose unfailingly cheerful assistance this book could never have been written. Other members of staff have been tremendously helpful during the long gestation period of this book, in particular Mrs Corinne Cherrad Marshall and Dennis Harrington. For the care and sensitivity shown by Michael Dudley, who took the photographs, the author records her thanks. For their support of the project, conceived by Timothy Wilson, the author wishes to record her debt to Geneviève Le Duc, Bernard Dragesco and Didier Cramoisan, John Whitehead, and especially to Rosalind Savill and John Mallet for their comments. The errors and omissions are of course the writer's own. Mr Martin Shopland generously paid for the conservation of certain pieces, so that they could be photographed for this book.

The Ashmolean Museum is grateful to the British Antique Dealers' Association, to the Ceramica-Stiftung, and to a benefactor who wishes to remain anonymous for financial help with the preparation and publication of this book; and to Christie's who generously supported the launch of the series to which this book belongs.

The book is dedicated to the late Tony Stevenson, much missed, a great lover of French porcelain, and with whom the writer often discussed the Ashmolean collection and his own.

Note
Unless described otherwise, all pieces are of artificial, or soft-paste porcelain (see p. 6); no. 10 was analysed by X-Ray diffraction by the Research Laboratory for Archaeology and the History of Art, Oxford University in November 1992. The body contains no mullite and is therefore a soft-paste porcelain of the glassy type containing the mineral wollastonite.

Auction sales cited are in London unless specified otherwise.

For the sake of clarity, all incised marks have been re-drawn by hand.

1   Cup and *trembleuse* saucer
Saint-Cloud, second quarter of the eighteenth
century

Moulded, cup supported in well of saucer with slightly
raised gallery in four parts.

The highly stylised flower pattern painted under
the glaze in blue derived from cobalt is typical of the
well-organised decorative schemes found on early
French porcelains. Cups and saucers like these enjoyed
decades of popularity and were probably in production
from the turn of the century to the 1740s, or even later.
The shape was once thought to have been made
specially for the sick or feeble, but it may in fact merely
have been one of the earliest Western types of porcelain
cup and saucer for tea. A variation on the form has an
unbroken gallery.[1]

The *SCT* mark may have been in use from 1722
when Henri Trou II became owner of the Saint-Cloud
factory after the death of his mother, Barbe Coudray,
who had inherited it from her husband, its founder, until
1755 or later.[2]

Marks: *t* surmounting *S.C* above *T* (marks on saucer), *S.C* sur-
mounting *T* above *f.* (marks on cup) both painted in underglaze-blue
H. of cup 6.9 cm.; d. of saucer 12.2 cm.
Bequeathed by L.R. Abel Smith, 1968.394.1 and 2

[1] Cf. Dawson, 1994, no.
5; another with the
SCT mark is no. 24
[2] See *ibid.*, pp 4–5

Painted mark

Painted mark

2 Toilet pot and cover
Saint-Cloud, second quarter of the eighteenth century

Thrown, the pattern of bamboo and rocks on one side and a banded hedge on the other painted over the glaze is characteristic of the earliest coloured decoration on Saint-Cloud porcelain. The pattern is copied from late-seventeenth century Japanese porcelains.

Experiments on enamel colours were under way at Saint Cloud by 1700 when an inventory was taken on the death of Henry Trou, but the colours were described as 'imperfect'. An advertisement shows that 'toutes sortes de couleurs' were in production by 1731. Two pots like these in the Louvre Museum have been recently dated c.1710–1720,[1] but this may be rather early for this style of painting.

Made in quantity at every French eighteenth-century porcelain factory (but not elsewhere in Europe), small face cream pots survive in a variety of decors. Saint-Cloud prunus-moulded and Mennecy painted examples are found in compartments bound with gold or silver thread in silk-lined boxes covered in tooled leather. They were bought by Paris merchants who had them mounted for wealthy French aristocrats.

[1] Guillebon, 1992, no. 4

Unmarked
H. incl. cover 6.1 cm.
Given by Cyril Andrade, 1968.260/1

3   Cane-handle
Saint-Cloud, about 1730

Moulded in two parts in *Tau* form, painted with stylised flowers and leaves, a butterfly, and a winged insect in the Chinese style. At each end is a red-brown chrysanthemum. The stick or cane fitted into the hollow stem.

Cane-handles were made in a profusion of shapes at Saint-Cloud.[1] The earliest are those with underglaze-blue decoration, such as the pommel-shaped cane-handle in the British Museum.[2] The painting on this coloured example, with its restricted range of overglaze enamels, made using metal oxides in a glassy matrix, represents the initial phase of coloured decoration when red-brown was often used for the outlines. In 1731 cane-handles in several forms were advertised by the Saint-Cloud factory operating from the rue Ville l'Evêque, Paris, and the advertisement was reissued in 1742, showing that there was a continuous demand.

Other similar cane-handles with different painted decors in the Chinese style were also made at Saint-Cloud.[3]

[1] A charming variant of this handle with a boar's head at one end is in the Musée des Arts Décoratifs, Paris, see Frégnac (ed.) 1964, p. 78
[2] Dawson, 1994, no. 9
[3] Illus. *Isaacson Collection*, 1989, no. 70

Unmarked
Max. h. 5.1 cm.; l. 10.5 cm.
Given by Cyril Andrade, 1968.263

4   Cup and saucer
Saint-Cloud, second quarter of the eighteenth
century

Moulded, the surface divided into panels by six depressions on the cup and on the saucer by five groups of two
depressions alternating with one. The pattern painted
over the glaze which includes bamboo, pine and prunus
growing by banded hedges is copied from eighteenth-
century Japanese Kakiemon porcelain.
    A variety of cups and saucers painted with this
pattern were made at Saint-Cloud, some without handles and others with handles and a gallery to hold the
cup.[1] A smaller size was also in production. They were
intended for tea, which was still costly and taken from
small cups. Unlike those in the East, these often had
handles. The painted pattern is also frequently seen on
many other pieces manufactured at Saint-Cloud (see no.
2) as well as on those made in the 1730s and 1740s at
Chantilly. It may also have been used at the Villeroy factory, precursor of Mennecy, which particularly favoured
oriental decoration.

[1] *Porcelain for Palaces*,
no. 313

Unmarked
H. of cup 6.9 cm.; d. of saucer 12.5 cm.
Given by Cyril Andrade, 1968.257/1 and 2

5 Teapot with silver mounts
Saint-Cloud, about 1730–40

Globular body and slightly domed lid ornamented with applied prunus branches, scrolled handle of baroque form grooved on outer surface. Circular hole inside pot for pouring.

The silver mount of the cover bears the fox head mark of the *sous-fermier* (tax official) Louis Robin in use between 1738–44,[1] implying that the teapot was mounted some time after it left the factory where it was made. The rather crudely-made silver finial is probably a replacement, as other similar teapots are garnished with button-shaped porcelain knops.[2] The rough surface underneath the finial shows that its was ground down to remove the remains of the original knop, which had probably been damaged.

[1] Nocq, H. *Le poinçon de Paris*, 1926–31, vol. iv, p. 233
[2] E.g. Victoria and Albert Museum, London, inv. no. C.131–1945

Bibliography: O. Impey, *Chinoiserie* London, 1977, p. 114, called 'a fairly close imitation of a blanc de chine original'

H. to top of cover 11.8 cm.
Unmarked
Purchased with the aid of the Friends of the Ashmolean, 1971.268
Comparable examples: *Isaacson Collection*, nos 57, 99 (attrib. to Mennecy); cf. Frégnac (ed.), 1964, p. 67

6   Wine-bottle cooler
Saint-Cloud, about 1730–40

Moulded, thickly potted. The rudimentary applied handles are in the form of grotesque heads with large ears and open mouths, their tongues showing. They and the Chinese style of the plant moulding suggest a date in the 1730s for the first appearance of this popular form of wine-bottle cooler, which would have held ice and was made in several different versions with varying moulded patterns.[1] On this version there are sunflowers flanking a leafy plant springing from mounds. Coolers were used on the table as part of the dessert service.

[1] Cf. Dawson, 1994, no. 12

Marks: *t* surmounting *SC* over *T* incised (see no. *1*)
D. 10.8 cm.
Given by Cyril Andrade, 1968.262

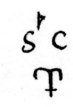

Incised mark

13

7 Candlestick group: *putai* seated by a tree surmounted by a bird
Saint-Cloud, about 1730–40

Modelled by hand and made in two parts, mounted with later gilt-bronze nozzles attached by means of a screw and washer. Concave base glazed underneath except on rim. Incised lines for veins of leaves and bird's feathers.

Probably one of the earliest groups made at the Saint-Cloud factory, it is perhaps not entirely successful. The proportions of bird and figure are unlikely and the leaves on the upper part of the tree-trunk below the branches do not quite disguise the join between the two parts of the group.

The small seated figure of *Pu-t'ai ho-shang*, a Chinese mendicant monk, said to be the incarnation of Amida Buddha, nestling between the roots of the tree-trunk, is known as a finial[1] and on another model of a candlestick.[2] The bird seems to be unique, although less ferocious birds surmount a pair of candlesticks (see note 2). An advertisement issued by the Saint-Cloud factory in 1731 shows that figures were on sale in the rue de la Madeleine, faubourg St. Honoré, Paris. Reprinted ten years later, it describes a variety of porcelain articles, including 'toutes sortes de figures Grotesques & Troncs d'Arbres, pour faire des Girandoles' (all sorts of grotesque figures and tree-trunks for candlesticks). *Grotesques* were usually figures in the oriental taste, fashionable in the second and third decades of the eighteenth century. A pair of glazed white candlestick groups with nozzles of porcelain[3] are in the same strange vein as this piece. Both seated figures, one of which is an oriental, have one hand across their body and the other resting on the head of a large creature, one rather like a lion, the other possibly a huge fish. These candlestick groups are the first efforts of the Saint-Cloud factory to combine figures based on oriental originals with candlesticks to make something which was intended to be useful as well as ornamental.

Bibliography: Dawson, 1993, p. 13, fig. 1

Unmarked
Restored. Leaf missing at putai's left and another leaf behind it broken at the base of the tree-trunk
H. 23 cm.
Given by Cyril Andrade, 1968.268

[1] On toilet-box
International Ceramics Fair and Seminar, Handbook, London, 1988, p. 52
[2] Cf. Drouot, Montaigne and Ferri, Paris, 15 November 1991, Lot 100, in colour on back cover of catalogue
[3] Fitzhenry sale, Paris, Drouot, 13–16 December 1909, Lot 208, called Saint-Cloud

8   Pot-pourri vase with a seated dog, lamb and lion
Saint-Cloud, about 1730–40

Vase and animals moulded, applied flowers modelled by hand, body pierced around shoulder with four groups of seven holes separated by depressions; triangular base modelled to resemble rockwork, underneath unglazed with four circular holes.

Vertical identations were used at Saint-Cloud to ornament vases, and, in different arrangements, on tobacco jars, cups and saucers and toilet pots. This was probably done by pressing the leather-hard clay into a mould.

The vase lacks its lid. It was used either as a perfume-burner for incense or for pot-pourri. Rosalind Savill[1] has re-published Madame Merigaud's mid-eighteenth century receipt for pot-pourri. As well as herbs, flowers and spices, such as white pepper, and lemon peel, the ingredients included waters (*eaux*), such as rosewater and *eau de reine de Hongrie*. Orange-flower water was used to prepare and refresh the pot-pourri. There were doubtless other less expensive pot-pourris, and the surviving number of pierced vases shows there was considerable demand for them.

Unmarked
H. 12.6 cm.
Bequeathed by L.R. Abel Smith, 1968. 396

[1] Savill, 1988, III, pp 1181–2, quoting L. Courajod, *Livre-Journal de Lazare-Duvaux, marchand-bijoutier ordinaire du roy 1748–58*, Paris, 1873, introduction

9 Toilet pot and cover (one of a pair)
Perhaps Bellevaux or another Paris factory, about 1720–30

Thrown, painted in underglaze-blue. Silver mount stamped with an indistinct mark.

Small pots like this, used for face cream, were made in quantity at every French porcelain factory in the first half of the eighteenth century. The dark blue rather crude painting of an unusual scroll, flower, scale and leaf pattern, as well as the thick walls of the pot, suggest that it may have been made in one of the Paris factories competing with Saint-Cloud in the 1720s and 1730s.[1]

Jean-Baptiste Bellevaux had a small kiln, in the rue Saint-Jacques. In 1715 various small pieces, including toilet pots, were seized by the authorities at the instigation of the Saint-Cloud factory owners, who had a royal monopoly on porcelain manufacture. A year later Bellevaux and another porcelain maker Antoine Pavie contested the seizure. They were unsuccessful, but may have continued their activities without marking their pieces so as to avoid detection. It is just possible that this may be an early product of the Saint-Cloud factory.

Unmarked
H. including cover 6 cm.
Given by Cyril Andrade, 1968.260/3 and 4

[1] For more detail about Bellevaux, see Dawson, 1994, p. 30; R. de Plinval de Guillebon, *Céramistes* and Guillebon, 1995

10 Group of a goat, kid and mastiff
Attributed to François Hébert, Paris, about 1741–55

Hollow, press-moulded. The dog, its mouth open and teeth bared in a growl, its short tail curled up, stands with its front legs stretched out across the circular base imitating rockwork. The goat perches over it, its front legs on the dog's back. The kid shelters under its mother's back legs, its left foreleg against her left rear flank, its rump against the dog's right shoulder.

This rare and lively group was conceived 'in the round', a feature most often found on figures made in the 1750s at Mennecy and Vincennes/Sèvres. The nearest parallel may be two fighting bulldogs modelled at Meissen by J. G. Kirchner before March 1733.[1]

Few pieces are known with this crossed arrows mark, long attributed to the Paris factory of François Hébert, but apparently never registered. Hébert married Marie-Anne Chicaneau, granddaughter of Barbe Coudray, widow of Pierre Chicaneau (died 1677), who leased the Saint-Cloud factory from Claude Révérend in 1674. Hébert, *maître faïencier* (master potter in tinglazed earthenware), is recorded in 1726[2] at 'la grande forge', rue du faubourg Saint-Antoine, Paris. In 1754 he went into partnership with Germain Desfarges, who had a faïence factory in the rue des Boulets. Hébert was declared bankrupt on 25 February 1755.[3] One of the group of Chicaneau descendants, he shared their 'secret' of porcelain-making from 1741, renewing the privilege in 1748 and 1752.

Hébert employed Gilles Dubois, who had stolen the secret of the Chantilly porcelain formula (for the paste) and taken it to Vincennes. He absconded in October 1752 and was arrested while working for Hébert who arranged his release, but in February 1753, himself laid charges against him.[4]

The factory also made small toilet pots,[5] meat-juice- or gravy-pots[6] and small cups.[7]

Bibliography: Comte X. de Chavagnac and Marquis de Grollier, *La Porcelaine Française*, Paris, 1906, p. 26; H.P. Fourest, 'Une porcelaine tendre d'Hébert dans les collections du Musée Céramique de Sèvres', *Faenza*, XL, 1954, pp. 37–39; Savage, 1960, Pl. 12; R. de Plinval de Guillebon, 'La porcelaine tendre à Paris au XVIIIe siècle', *Publications of the French Porcelain Society*, XI, 1994, p. 28 no. 11

Mark: crossed arrows painted in underglaze-blue
H. 19.5 cm.
Goat's horns, ears and tail restored
Given by Cyril Andrade, 1968.267
Formerly the comte de Chavagnac collection, sold Paris, Drouot, 19–21 June 1911, Lot 21[8]

[1] Cf. J. Willisberger and R. Rückert, *Meissener Porzellan des 18. Jahrhunderts,* Dortmund, 1982, p. 139
[2] G. Le Duc and R. de Plinval de Guillebon, 'Contribution à l'étude de la manufacture de faïence et de porcelaine de Saint-Cloud pendant ses cinquante premières années', *Keramik-Freunde der Schweiz, Mitteilungsblatt*, 105, March 1991, pp. 3–53; R. de Plinval de Guillebon, 1995, p. 56
[3] See R. de Plinval de Guillebon, *Céramistes*
[4] See N. Ballu, 'La carrière des Dubois', *Cahiers de la Céramique et des Arts du feu*, 10, 1958, pp. 92–3, source Dossier de Gilles Dubois, Bibliothèque de l'Arsenal, mss 11.780, 11.780.2
[5] Inv. no. MNCS 13344, 13342, the larger toilet-pot lacks its cover and is poorly potted and unevenly glazed
[6] Reg. No. VAM C. 511–1909; Musée National de Céramique, Sèvres, inv. no. 13345
[7] Musée National de Céramique, Sèvres, inv. no. 13341
[8] Sold to Argiropoulo for 510 francs, restored, according to note in catalogue in British Museum, Department of Medieval and later Antiquities

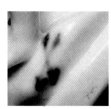

Painted mark

11   Bowl with shaped rim
Chantilly, about 1735-40

Moulded, painted over the tin glaze when it had dried but before firing with a pattern copied from Japanese Kakiemon porcelains. The shaped rim is found on Japanese hexagonal bowls.

Larger bowls of similar form painted with Kakiemon-style patterns were made at Chantilly to serve as wine-bottle coolers,[1] but the purpose of this small bowl remains uncertain. The form was probably copied from a Meissen bowl,[2] or possibly from its Japanese forebear.

Unmarked
H. 5.4 cm.; l. 8 cm.
Given by Cyril Andrade, 1968.197

[1] Ader, Picard, Tajan, Paris, Hôtel George V, 11 March 1991, Lots 29, 30. Cf. Munger *et al.*, *The Forsyth Wickes Collection in the Museum of Fine Arts Boston*, Boston, 1992, no. 163; Coutts 1991, p. 81, fig. 4
[2] E. Lassen, *Die Sammlung David, Meissen Porzellan*, Copenhagen, 1985, p. 134, no. 51

12   Drug jar and cover
Chantilly, about 1750

This type of soft-paste porcelain thrown drug jar of undulating form with a tin glaze, painted with flowers in the Kakiemon style and with a wreath of leaves and berries and reeds (which in this instance does not enclose the name of a drug) is a fairly common survival. Examples in public collections,[1] and on the market,[2] suggest that they were sold in quantity to pharmacies. The decoration is meticulously painted, the brown carefully outlined in manganese and the knop coloured blue.

Jars like these were made in at least two sizes.[3] The French names of the drugs were probably painted on after the jars left the factory.

Bibliography: O. Impey, *Chinoiserie,* London, 1977, Pl. 108

Mark: hunting horn painted in red
H. including cover 15.1 cm.
Given by Cyril Andrade, 1968.205/1 & 2

[1] Cf. Dawson, 1994, no. 43
[2] Sold by Perrin-Reyere-Lajeunesse, Hôtel des Chevaux Légers, Versailles, 22 March 1992, Lots 115–117
[3] Musée National de Céramique, Sèvres, inv. nos 21526/1 and 2 and 7778, each painted with the name of a different drug

Painted mark

Painted mark

13   Jug and cover
Chantilly, about 1735–40

Thrown, painted over the tin glaze with a banded hedge and squirrel pattern based on a Japanese Kakiemon original in which the squirrel is a tree rat.[1] Green scroll pattern on inexpertly applied strap handle. Silver mount.

The glaze on this piece is poorly applied leaving some areas uncovered. The handle is not straight, possibly indicating an early date of production. The finely-made finial with its three petals and stalk is typical of the factory.

The jug was perhaps for oil or vinegar, but no comparable shaped piece is known from any other French factory.

Unmarked; mount unmarked
H. 14.5 cm.
Given by Cyril Andrade, 1968.188

[1] *Porcelain for Palaces*, no. 315

14 Flared dish
Chantilly, perhaps 1735–40

Thrown. The function of this dish is unclear, but it may have been intended for use at table. It precedes the appearance of porcelain dinner and dessert services in France in the early 1750s. Its stiff painting of a banded hedge, prunus tree and chrysanthemum spray in a pale palette, as well as its simple shape, point to an early date of production. The brown rim is probably copied from a Japanese prototype, and no counterpart was made by any of its competitors.

Mark: hunting horn painted in red
H. 4.9 cm.; d. 14.3 cm.
Given by Cyril Andrade, 1968.198

Painted mark

15   Saucer
Chantilly, about 1735

Thrown, painted over the tin glaze with one of the most charming of all the early Chantilly patterns inspired by Japanese Kakiemon porcelains. The brown-painted rim may well predate the introduction of gilding at Chantilly; it too is based on Japanese porcelains.

A teapot painted with the same scene is known[1] suggesting that matching tewares were made.

[1] Mrs H. Dupuy sale, Parke-Bernet, New York, 2 and 3 April 1948, Lot 102

Unmarked (the mark has apparently been scratched off)
D. 12.5 cm.
Purchased with a contribution from the MGC/V&A Fund, 1976.74; formerly Mr and Mrs W. Sainsbury Collection

16 Jug
Chantilly, about 1740–50

Thrown. Although the form, which should once have had a lid,[1] is purely Western, the decoration of the so-called 'banded hedge and squirrel pattern' painted over the tin glaze is in the Japanese Kakiemon style.

This covered jug was presumably intended to hold a warm drink. The closest comparable piece made at another factory is a Vincennes porcelain covered *marmite*, or stewpot, or *pot à bouillon* (brothpot) on three feet dating from around 1744–48[2] copied from a Meissen original made in the 1730s.[3] As the Vincennes factory employed several workmen who had been at Chantilly, there may be a link between the two factories and their products.

Mark: hunting horn painted in red
H. 11.1 cm.
Given by Cyril Andrade, 1968.200

[1] A complete example with a slightly domed lid surmounted by a typical Chantilly finial consisting of three petals is in the Musée des Arts Décoratifs, Paris, inv. 35397
[2] Préaud and d'Albis, 1991, no. 85, p. 141
[3] *Meissener Porzellan*, 1966, no. 294

Painted mark

17   Two-handled cup
Chantilly, about 1745–50

Thrown, painted over the tin glaze in the Kakiemon style with stylised chrysanthemums, leaves and a rock. The rim is painted brown to imitate oriental porcelains and there are orange-red scrolls on the handles. The wrinkled glaze on the base has 'crawled', perhaps because the surface of the unglazed piece was greasy.

This large flared cup, which should have a cover and a stand, is similar to the form in production at Vincennes as early as 1752 and known as a milk cup.[1] It is difficult to know whether the Chantilly cup predates the Vincennes one. The tin-glaze, the oriental style of the painted rock and chrysanthemums and the wheatsheaf pattern suggest a date before 1750, but both concerns were filling a common need and their milk cups are probably more or less contemporaneous.

Unmarked
H. 9.4 cm.
Given by G.R. Reitlinger, 1978.299; sold Sotheby's, 2 February 1965, lot 65

[1] Préaud and d'Albis, 1991, p. 157, no. 132; cf. Dawson, 1994, no. 97

18   Spittoon
Chantilly, 1740–45

Thrown, tin glaze with several bare patches. The painted decoration derives from eighteenth-century Japanese Kakiemon porcelain.[1]

Louis-Henri, Duke of Bourbon, and Prince of Condé, known as Monsieur Le Duc (1692–1740), founder of the factory, amassed a vast collection of oriental works of art, including porcelain from Japan.[2] Spittoons painted in underglaze-blue were made there around 1700 for export to the West[3] and may have inspired the Chantilly factory. Villeroy-Mennecy also made spittoons.[4]

Two models of spittoon were made at about this time at Vincennes. The first was in production by autumn 1752, the second by 1756.[5]

Spittoons of this form were made in England, for example at the Lowestoft factory.[6]

Unmarked
H. 7.3 cm.; d. of top part 11.8 cm.
Purchased with a contribution from the MGC/V&A Fund, 1976.73; formerly Mr and Mrs W. Sainsbury collection
Comparable examples: Mrs H. Dupuy sale, Parke-Bernet, New York, 3 April 1948, Lot 285

[1] See *Porcelain for Palaces*, no. 315
[2] For a discussion of oriental decoration at Chantilly see G. Le Duc, 'Chantilly, un certain regard vers l'Extrême Orient 1730–50', Publications of the French Porcelain Society, London, X, 1993
[3] I am grateful to Oliver Impey for his opinion on this spittoon
[4] Dupont, 1987, p. 61, fig. 4; C. Dauguet and D. Guillemé-Brulon, *La porcelaine française*, Paris, n.d., p. 23
[5] Porcelaines de Vincennes, 1977–78, p. 45
[6] B. Watney *English Blue and White Porcelain of the Eighteenth Century*, London, repr. 1979, Pl. 82E

19 Hanging flower vase
Chantilly, about 1740–50

Moulded, waisted with a central ridge; back and base unglazed except for a few splashes; top pierced by numerous circular oval holes for the display of cut flowers except along the back edge; semi-circular hole near the back in the centre probably for filling with water. The flange at the centre back has two circular holes for suspension, showing that it was intended to be hung on a wall.

Although the overglaze painted decoration of the so-called banded hedge pattern, accompanied by scattered flowers in the oriental style and insects, is typical of Chantilly in the 1740s, this rare form is rather sophisticated. White porcelain examples with applied flower decoration are also known.[1] It may be based on a tin-glazed earthenware (faïence) version.

Mark: hunting horn painted in red
Max. h. 11.3 cm.; max. l. 16 cm.
Restoration to front edge
Given by Cyril Andrade, 1968.201
Bibliography: Savage, 1960, Pl. 19b

[1]Cf. Unpainted pair with relief decoration, same size as Ashmolean example, Christner sale, Christie's, New York, Vol. III Important French Porcelain, 9 June 1979, Lot 171 and see Lot 156

20 Tureen and cover
Chantilly, about 1750

Thrown, mastiff's head handles, their open mouths showing palate and tongue, separately moulded and attached with liquid clay before firing.

The decoration, closely based on Japanese porcelains, includes chrysanthemums and quails and a butterfly and a flowering spray with two ears of millet, on one of which perches an insect. Near the border are two quails and a 'cracked ice' pattern.

This tureen was evidently part of a dinner service but no matching soup plates or dishes are known. Two wine-coolers with dog's head handles, painted with oriental motifs below a similar border are perhaps related.[1]

A similar tureen[2] may be the Ashmolean one rather than a second piece.

Mark: hunting horn painted in red
D. of bowl 26.4 cm.
Replacement finial; one handle restored
Given by Messrs S.J. Phillips and Winifred Williams, 1980.1; F. Halinbourg collection, Paris, 1913, no. 152; Mrs H. Dupuy sale, Parke-Bernet, New York, 2, 3 April 1948, Lot 387
Exh. Pavillon de Marsan, Paris, 'La porcelaine française de 1673 à 1914', 1929, No. 1813; Winifred Williams, London, 6–27 June 1974, 'The Kakiemon Influence on European Porcelain', no. 9, and 3–20 July 1978, '18th Century French Porcelain' no. 73; *Porcelain for Palaces*, 1990, no. 365

[1] Sold Christie's, 25 June 1963, René Fribourg Collection: I, Lot 38
[2] N. Ballu, *La Porcelaine Française*, Paris, n.d., Pl. 8

21 Gravy pot and cover
Chantilly, about 1750

Thrown, painted over the tin glaze with a stylised flower and insect pattern derived from Japanese Kakiemon porcelain; ear-shaped handle and button knop painted in iron red, the first with a scroll pattern; rim of pot painted brown in imitation of oriental porcelains.

Pots like these were used in eighteenth-century France at table for serving the meat juices accompanying the meat course. In contemporary England rather similar pots were called 'custard cups' and were part of the dessert service. French examples from all the big porcelain factories survive. On the evidence of a lead-glazed spirally-moulded example dating from around 1765-70 in the Ashmolean,[1] they continued in production at Chantilly for around twenty years.

The rather free painting of this example, which is not strictly oriental, together with the swelling shape, which has nothing in common with oriental porcelains, and the palette of colours used, (two colours of green, yellow and manganese) is evidence that the piece was not made in the factory's first phase of activity.

[1] WA 1968.191 (lacking cover, blue sprigs underglaze-blue horn mark)

Unmarked
H. 9.1 cm.
Given by Cyril Andrade, 1968.1 and 2

22   Wine-glass cooler
Chantilly, about 1745–50

Thrown, painted over the tin glaze with the banded hedge and squirrel pattern, also found on *16*; applied angular handles painted manganese purple, pale green leaf terminals embellished with pale yellow flowers.

For commentary, see page opposite.

H. 10 cm.
Mark: hunting horn painted in red
Given by Cyril Andrade, 1968.202

Painted mark

23   Wine-glass cooler
Chantilly, about 1750–55

Thrown, painted over the tin glaze in seven colours with a flower and leaf pattern in the oriental style; rim painted brown in imitation of oriental porcelains; applied twig handles painted manganese brown, stylised leaf and flower terminals.

A wide range of sizes of thrown vessels with a variety of applied handles and differing decorative schemes was made at Chantilly over a period of several decades for serving wine at the dining table.[1] The Vincennes/ Sèvres factory records show that wine-glass coolers were part of the second or dessert service. The glass was cooled with the bowl resting in ice. This cooler was made during the second decade of the Chantilly factory's existence when the oriental style was giving way to a European type of flower-painting typified by *25*. At the same time the number of colours available to the porcelain painter was growing. Here manganese oxide was used to make purple for the handles.

[1] Malgras (ed.), 1983, p. 20, 22, 25, 26, 40, 54, 58, 60, 66 illustrates some of the many versions of the wine-cooler in the Musée Condé, Chantilly

Marks: hunting horn painted in red
H. 10.8 cm.
Given by Cyril Andrade, 1968.203

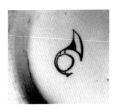

Painted mark

33

24 Sugar bowl, cover and stand
Chantilly, about 1750

Moulded, cover relief-moulded with four large and four smaller leaves; painted over tin glaze with stylised leaves and chrysanthemums, insects in the Kakiemon style; brown rim to the stand imitating oriental porcelain. Matching spoon lacking.

This elaborate form, probably intended for use in the dessert course and characteristic of Chantilly, was evidently popular as it stayed in production with adaptations until well into the period when the factory had adopted European-style decoration (see *27*).

H. of bowl and cover 10.2 cm.; l. of stand 22.3 cm.
Mark: hunting horn painted in red on stand and bowl
Given by Cyril Andrade, 1968.195
Small chips to stand

Painted mark

25 Two-handled broth bowl and cover *(écuelle)*
Chantilly, about 1755–60

Painted over the tin glaze with naturalistic European flowers including daffodils, forget-me-nots, an iris, a honeysuckle and peonies, probably based on engravings; baroque-style scroll handles each painted with two flowers; rose finial on domed cover undecorated; green leaves at its base veined in brown.

This pot is more likely to be for broth, often taken during the *toilette* which lasted several hours in the morning, than to hold sugar. It has no hole for a spoon and is rather larger than most sugar bowls except for lobed examples made at Chantilly, Mennecy and Sèvres.[1] Whatever its use, it may have once had a matching stand, although surviving examples do not.

[1] Sold Paris, Ader Tajan, Hôtel George V, 21 June 1993 (Deleplanque Collection), Lots 97, 98, 99, 100, 101

H. including cover: 12.5 cm.
Mark: hunting horn painted in red
Given by Cyril Andrade, 1968.190, 1 and 2
Collection label embossed in red *LUIS D'AGUIAR COLLECTION NO* and inscribed in ink *57* and *sucrier couvert*
Comparable examples: A rather similar pot and cover without stand but with a different knop (the three-petalled type frequently found on Chantilly wares), red hunting horn mark, h. 15.5 cm., was with Armin B. Allen, London, in June 1989, see *Isaacson Collection*, no. 76; another without stand and with overglaze-blue painted landscape and flowers, bud knop, sold Paris, Ader Tajan, Hôtel George V, 21 June 1993, Lot 124

Painted mark

26 Jug
Chantilly, about 1760

Moulded in the form of a barrel with five hoops and with indentations representing the staves; flattened scroll handle, out-turned at lower end; upper part moulded with a leaf with 'kick' at the top. The scattered flower decoration painted over the tin glaze overlaps the realistically painted 'staves' in more than one place; rim painted brown, in imitation of oriental porcelains.

This pleasing, and apparently rather rare,[1] jug is one of a series of pieces made at Chantilly in the form of barrels. Although other factories were inspired by the barrel form, none copied it quite so closely.

Marks: hunting horn painted in red; paper label inscribed in ink *1–157 RE/Chantilly*
H. 15 cm.
Given by Cyril Andrade, 1968.189
Lower part of handle restored, lip restored, slight chips to foot

[1] Only three other examples have been traced:
a) Bowes Museum, Barnard Castle, Co. Durham, Coutts, 1991, p. 83, fig. 7
b) sold Perrin-Reyere-Lajeunesse, Hôtel des Chevaux-Légers, Versailles, 22 March 1992, Lot 46
c) sold Ader Tajan, Hôtel George V, Paris, 29 June 1994, Lot 32

Painted mark

27 Sugar bowl, cover and stand
Chantilly, about 1760

The form of this charmingly painted lead-glazed sugar
bowl, cover and stand clearly represents a development
of the earlier model (see *24*), whilst the decoration has
followed the evolution of taste evident in porcelain from
all over Europe. Large 'European style' flowers were
particularly popular on Meissen porcelain, and it is
likely that Chantilly was trying to make a rival French
product to appeal to this luxury market in exactly
the same way as Vincennes had done in the late 1740s
and early 1750s. These flowers too, like those painted
on Vincennes white-ground porcelains (see *42*, for
example), were probably based on as yet untraced
engravings.

There is no gilding on the pieces as this would
have contravened the monopoly of the royal factory at
Sèvres, but the red-brown rim is a successful substitute.

The spoon is missing.

Mark: hunting horn painted in red
H. of bowl 16 cm.; l. 24.1 cm.
Bequeathed by L.R. Abel Smith, 1968.399.1, 2 and 3

Painted mark

28　Two-handled sauceboat
Chantilly, about 1760–70

Moulded, grooved handles and flared foot; painted over the lead glaze in blue with stylised flowering branches. Rims painted blue. Form based on a French silver shape.

Sauceboats were made in many different shapes and sizes in eighteenth-century France, as in England. The Sèvres version, introduced in 1756, is similar but has lobes.[1]

Blue flowers, painted either over or under the glaze, were the mainstay of the Chantilly production in the 1760s and 1770s. At this period it made domestic wares in quantity, to judge from what survives. At least four different patterns were in production, several of them rather more elaborate than that found on this sauceboat, which is, however, skilfully executed. Patterns like these were copied in England, particularly at Caughley, Shropshire in the late 1770s and 1780s, often on shapes that were also based on French models.[2]

Marks: hunting horn painted in underglaze-blue; *co* (?) *ucon* incised
L. 21.9 cm.
Bequeathed by L.R. Abel Smith, 1968.398.1

[1] A finely-painted example from the service presented by the French King to Prince Starhemberg is illus. Savill, 1994, p. 25, fig. 1
[2] Wine glass cooler illus. B. Watney, *English Blue and White Porcelain of the Eighteenth Century*, London, repr. 1979, Pl. 89B

Painted mark

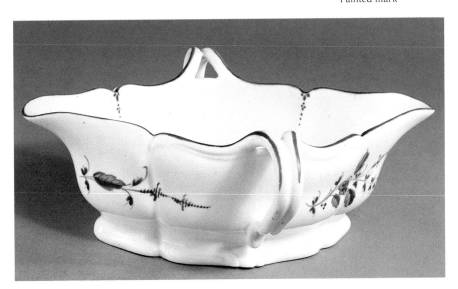

29   Snuff-box
Chantilly, about 1750–60

Cover moulded with the bust of a man and woman wearing sleeping caps, their bodies underneath a sheet and coverlet. Tin glazed. The wheatsheaf pattern is painted on the underside of the lid, which is flat; inside of box decorated with flowers in the oriental style. Unmarked silver-gilt mount.

This amusing and original box is one of a series of idiosyncratic boxes for snuff, bonbons, or face patches made at Chantilly. Many of these are in the form of animals, such as cats.

The Ashmolean collection includes twenty-nine boxes from a group of French soft-paste porcelain factories, which in the present state of our knowledge are not always easy to attribute.

Mark: hunting horn painted in red inside box
H. 4.1 cm.; l. 7.8 cm.
Cover and one corner restored
Given by Cyril Andrade, 1968.156; sold Sotheby's 27 February 1966, Lot 38
Comparable examples: Musées Royaux d'art et d'histoire, Brussels, illus. Beaucamp-Markowsky, 1985, no. 399

30 Snuff-box
Chantilly, about 1750

The painting on this splendid box, which is over a tin glaze, is of exceptional quality. The scenes, in particular the one on the front of a snake and a mongoose at the right facing a cockatrice, its wings outstretched, conjures up a vision of Cathay, the exotic Orient as seen by Europeans. The box is typical of high-quality pieces made in the 1750s at Chantilly at the moment it came in competition with the royal factory. Vincennes/Sèvres never seems to have seriously engaged in the trade in *objets de vertu*, that is all sorts of small articles such as boxes. However, its gradual inroad on the market for luxury porcelain threatened the very existence of the Chantilly concern.

Unmarked
H. 4 cm.; l. of cover: 7.5 cm.
Given by Cyril Andrade, 1968.155

41

31 Figure of *putai* holding a fan standing next to a jar
Chantilly, about 1740

Hollow, press-moulded; base partly covered with a tin glaze. For *Pu-t'ai ho-shang*, see 7.

The figure was probably intended for mounting in gilt-bronze and to take the place of an oriental ivory, soapstone or *blanc de chine* porcelain (Fukien, China) example. It may have been destined for a mantelpiece or for a shelf as an ornament, and the jar, which in the Chinese original was a begging bowl, may perhaps been a vase for flowers. Such pieces were presumably made for a luxury market, but at present no details are available about their selling price. Its humour is typical of many of the figures in the oriental idiom made at the Chantilly factory.

H. 22.8 cm.
Unmarked
Vase cracked and chipped
Given by Cyril Andrade, 1968.273; Sotheby's, 26 November 1968, Lot 66
Comparable examples: Musée des Arts Décoratifs, Paris, illus. Frégnac (ed.), 1964, p. 97 (coloured version)

32 Figure of a vegetable seller (*Hotteuse*)
Chantilly, about 1740–50

Moulded, hollow, flat base with touches of glaze and brown patches. She wears a cap, a low-cut dress with tight overjacket, long sleeves and an overskirt. Over her shoulders are straps holding a basket, the base of which she supports at the back with her left hand. The basket is empty and the inside of the figure is visible.

This figure was a popular model and is usually sold with a male Oriental companion.[1] Coloured versions are known.[2] The model is probably based on a Meissen figure by J. J. Kändler first recorded in 1741,[3] although the Chantilly *hotteuse* is in an inventory taken in 1741 on the death of the second Duchess of Bourbon, Caroline of Hesse-Rheinfeld.[4] It was 'pirated' by the Villeroy/Mennecy factory. Their smaller version may have been moulded directly from the Chantilly figure.[5] It was made in tin-glazed earthenware at the Strasbourg factory.[6]

Unmarked
H. 28 cm.
Given by Cyril Andrade, 1968.206

[1] Uncoloured pair, their panniers pierced for flowers, illus. Coutts, 1991, p. 80, fig. 1; white pair illus. Malgras (ed.), 1983, pp. 14–15; pair Christner sale Vol. III, Christie's, New York, 9 June 1979, Lot 172
[2] Victoria and Albert Museum, London, inv. no. 392-1909 (male figure), 393-1909 (same model as this)
[3] N. Ballu, 'Influence de l'Extrême-Orient sur le style de Chantilly au XVIIIe siècle', *Cahiers de la Céramique*, 11, 1958, p. 111, fig. 17
[4] Coutts, *ibid*
[5] Ballu, *op. cit.*, p. 110, fig. 15, 16 shows both, the Mennecy one measuring 26 cm
[6] J. Chompret *et al.*, *Répertoire de la Faïence Française*, Paris 1933, 8 vols, Pls 9C, D

33   Pair of figures of dwarfs
Mennecy, about 1750–60

Press-moulded, hollow, highly translucent; unexplained discolouration around nose, right hand and feet of male dwarf; firecrack across his right cheek; faint splash of blue below his left arm indicating that cobalt was being used for underglaze-blue decoration. The rockwork base of the female dwarf is characteristic of the Mennecy factory.

Several eighteenth-century porcelain factories in the German-speaking lands, as well as in Venice (Cozzi factory) and Florence (Doccia factory) made dwarfs.[1] In England dwarfs were made at the Chelsea factory from about 1751.[2] In France, only Villeroy-Mennecy made dwarfs, known in at least six different models.[3] No engraving in J. Callot's *Il Callotto resuscitato oder neu eingerichtes Zwerchen cabinet* (Amsterdam, 1716 edition) corresponds exactly with these figures, and they must be based on other prints in circulation at that time.

[1] G Morrazzoni, *Le Porcellane italiane*, Milan, 1960, vol. I, Tav. 85, 95c and L. G. Lisci, *la Porcellana di Doccia*, Milan, 1963, fig. 39
[2] F. Severne Mackenna, *Chelsea Porcelain, the Triangle and Raised Anchor Wares*, Leigh-on-Sea, 1948, pl. 39, fig. 80 (raised red anchor)
[3] *Linsky collection, op.cit.*, Nos. 281-4, 286

Bibliography: Savage, 1960, Pl. 30b; Dawson, 1993, fig. 2

Unmarked
H. 14 cm. (male figure), 13.3 cm.
Given by Cyril Andrade, 1968.265,266
Comparable examples: male dwarf illus. in *The Jack and Belle Linksy Collection in the Metropolitan Museum of Art, Porcelains*, entry by C. Le Corbeiller, New York, 1984, no. 281

34   Pair of barking mastiffs
Mennecy, perhaps about 1750–55

Probably moulded. Unglazed flat bases. Dog with pink collar and yellow buckle, bitch with blue collar with a yellow buckle.

The models, which are a true pair as they face each other, are otherwise unrecorded. These mastiffs seem to have no direct prototype at the Meissen factory in Saxony,[1] as one might have expected. They are not easily datable since no precise chronology of Mennecy has yet been established. The technical problem of supporting the body of a prancing animal has been solved in exactly the same way on a pair of horses, one of which bears the incised mark *DV* used by the Mennecy factory.[2]

As at Meissen, a range of animal figures was made and they were evidently popular.[3]

Unmarked
Both mastiffs restored
H. 12.5 cm.; l. of base of dog looking right 8.7 cm.
Given by Cyril Andrade, 1968.255/1 and 2; probably sold Sotheby's, 13 November 1951, Lot 126, £180 to Lester

[1] See K. Albiker, *Die Meissner Porzellantiere im 18. Jahrhundert*, Berlin, 1935, including seated snarling she-wolf with two cubs, Pl. XXXIX, no. 158
[2] Christner Collection, Christie's, New York, Vol. III, French Porcelain, 9 June 1979, Lot 163
[3] Different models of Mennecy dog and bitch, L. 6.5 cm. see Winifred Williams, London, *An Exhibition of 18th Century French Porcelain*, 3–20 July 1978, no 59

35 Pair of finches
Mennecy, about 1760

Moulded, bases flat and unglazed; painted over the lead glaze in a palette of five colours, including pink, a colour much used at Mennecy.

Bird figures like these were sometimes fixed to waisted pedestals.[1] They are invariably made with the bird's legs straddling a tree-trunk which supports the body, and are carefully painted. Probably intended as table-decoration, they exhibit the liveliness often found in Mennecy birds and animals.

Vincennes produced versions from 1749[2] and the records mention parrots, bullfinches, swans, tits, canaries and goldfinches. All these were probably inspired by the birds made at Meissen, which were intended to be ornithologically correct.

[1]Cf. Frégnac (ed.), 1983, p. 113, 116, 121
[2]Préaud and d'Albis, 1991, p. 170

Unmarked
H. 8.8 cm. and 8.2 cm.
Tails restored. Firecrack disguised by green painted decoration on base of 1968.253/2
Given by Cyril Andrade, 1968.253/1 and 2; Sotheby's, 23 November 1968, Lot 62

36   Figure of a goat
Mennecy, about 1755–60

Probably moulded, painted over the lead glaze in a restricted palette of colours typical of the Mennecy factory.

This figure is one of a series of small-scale animals and birds probably made in imitation of Meissen figures. It may have been intended as table-decoration, or might have been mounted in gilt-bronze as an ornament.

The earliest figure-production at Mennecy ranges from rather crude figures reminiscent in form and colouring of those made at Stratford-le-Bow, London, around 1750 which are attributed to the so-called 'Muses Modeller', to rather lively animal and bird subjects – the animals often in action. Another group of finely-modelled figures, often depicting trades and usually left undecorated to show the sparkling white colour of the porcelain, are probably slightly later in date as they are altogether more sophisticated in conception and execution.

Mark: D.V. incised in concave depression underneath
H. 8.5 cm.
Ears and horns restored
Given by Cyril Andrade, 1968.254

Incised mark

37   Group of a pleading lover or the music lesson
Mennecy, probably about 1760

Hollow, press-moulded.

Figures and groups made at Mennecy, whether incised with the factory mark *DV* or not, are of widely varying quality. There are several which are crudely formed like this one, usually with gallant subjects (this one may be theatrical) painted with scattered flowers on a white ground in colours which are characteristic of Mennecy. A figure of a seated Chinaman, once in the Firestone Collection[1] is probably part of this production.

There is another group in the Ashmolean depicting seated lovers with a birdcage which is attributed to the Mennecy factory. However its origin has been questioned.[2]

Unmarked
Max. 19.5 cm.
The girl's head may have been repaired. The slight yellowish discolouration of the glaze is often a sign of decaying adhesive. His left arm is repaired
Given by Cyril Andrade, 1968.252. As no other example has been discovered, this one, described as having the head restuck, may have been the one sold from the comte de Chavagnac collection, Drouot, Paris, 19–21 June 1911, Lot 205, 2200 francs (buyer unknown)

[1] See R. Berges, 'Mennecy porcelains from the Elizabeth Parke Firestone collection', *Connoisseur*, 170, 1969, p. 253, fig. 16
[2] WA 1968.251; Cf. Dawson, 1994, p. 63

38   Figure of a girl holding her skirt
Mennecy, perhaps about 1765–70

Moulded, glazed. Flat unglazed base with some dis-colourations.

This figure has in the past been attributed to the Saint-Cloud factory, probably because the incised factory mark is barely visible. However, the very white porcelain is typical of one phase of the Mennecy factory, presumably not long before its closure in 1773. The fine crisp modelling, particularly of the delicate bows on the sleeves and hair, the rosettes on the shoes, and the slight turn of the head are all characteristic features of a style and a high level of skill which cannot yet be attributed to any particular workman.

Mark: *DV* incised on top of the rockwork base at the back on the left
H. 21.5 cm.
Damage to the left of overskirt
Bequeathed by L.R. Abel Smith, 1968.397

Incised mark

52

39   Triple salt
Bourg-la-Reine, about 1773–80

Moulded, handle imitating basketwork, motif repeated around the rim; painted over the lead glaze in rather dry colours.

Triple salts, first made at the Vincennes porcelain factory, forerunner of Sèvres, from at least as early as 1752,[1] continued to be popular, and were made in hard-paste porcelain at the Boissettes factory just outside Paris around 1775-1780.[2]

Salts, of which a large variety of the single form were made from the first decade of the eighteenth century,[3] were used during the first, or dinner, service for celery, garlic and sea salt. This Bourg-la-Reine version was doubtless cheaper by far than its Vincennes/Sèvres counterpart. Not all services included single salts, double salts and triple salts. The service presented to Prince Starhemberg, now at Waddesdon Manor,[4] a reward for the negotiation of the marriage between Marie-Antoinette, daughter of the Empress of Austria and Louis XV's grandson, was particularly grand and expensive and so had all three kinds.

Bourg-la-Reine, in effect the continuation of the Villeroy/Mennecy factory, operated between late 1772 and around 1805 when it was sold. Apart from some complex figure groups, it made mostly small pieces. Other service pieces such as tureens are almost unknown, perhaps because the workmen were relatively unskilled.

Max. h. 8 cm.
Mark: *BR* incised (indistinct)
Bequeathed by L.R. Abel Smith, 1968.404

[1] The Vincennes factory inventory dated October 1752 includes two glazed salts *à/en trois marrons* valued at 24 *livres*. Two *salières à trois compartiments* are in the kiln records under the date 1 February 1754. Madame Préaud, archivist of the Sèvres factory, kindly supplied these references
[2] Guillebon, 1992, no. 20
[3] Cf. Dawson, 1994, nos 3, 4, pp. 8–9
[4] Savill, 1994, pp. 25–33

40 Vase with applied flowers (vase Duplessis à fleurs balustre rocaille)
Vincennes, 1749–52

Moulded, eight-lobed shell-moulded foot, handles formed of four thin ropes of clay entwined at lower end issuing from four different applied flower sprays on stems. Some small patches unglazed, perhaps because of a poorly-fitting glaze. Rich gilding, the flowers carefully tooled.

Vases like this, designed by Jean-Claude Duplessis, were in production in seven sizes by the time of the factory's first inventory, which is dated October 1752. This is the smallest size, and was probably part of a *garniture* of three or five vases, perhaps for a mantelpiece. Examples can be found in many collections.[1]

The Vincennes factory records show that flowers were produced very early on in quantity. It is interesting to see them used here applied on one of the factory's own vases, rather than mounted on metal stems as they often were.

Unmarked
H. 10 cm.
Given by Cyril Andrade, 1968.275

[1] For a *garniture* of three see Préaud and d'Albis, 1991, p. 131, no. 63; like the examples in the Victoria and Albert Museum, London, inv. C. 357 to 9-1909, the foot differs; one illus. Honey, 1950, Pl. 52

41   Pair of glass-coolers (*seaux à verre ordinaires*)
Vincennes, 1749–53

Moulded, handles in the form of interlocking twigs with leaf terminals. The painted decoration on a white ground enclosed within shaped reserves outlined with thick gilt lines is characteristic of the early period of the factory.

[1] Biographical details given by Savill, 1988, vol. III, pp. 1068–9

Coolers of four different sizes were produced at the Vincennes factory from its earliest years for wine-bottles, half-bottles, liqueur-bottles and glasses. They were made in various shapes and with decoration ranging from figure scenes in the Meissen manner, maritime, landscape and allegorical scenes, scenes after Boucher, with bird, floral and relief decoration.

The factory inventory of 1752 lists moulds for this form. The sale price for examples with landscape decoration was 18 *livres*. These coolers must date from between 1749, when gilding was introduced, and 1753, when date-letters were first used as part of the factory mark.

Marks: interlaced *LL*s with dots above and below (without dots on 1948.158.1) enclosing painter's mark of Vincent Taillandier[1]
H. 10.3 cm.; d. 11.1 cm. (1948.158.6 1); h. 10.4 cm. (1948.158.6 2)
Bequeathed by Sir B. Eckstein Bt., 1948.158.6. 1 & 2
Foot of 1948.158.6.1 restored, rim of 1948.158.6. 2 restored

Painted mark

42 Chamberpot (pot de chambre forme de limasson)
Vincennes, about 1751-1752

Moulded with snail-form whorls near the handle, which simulates a branch, but is painted pink and gilt; flat, unglazed base. Painted with four groups of flowers, including daffodils and cornflowers, and with a dragonfly.

The form, clearly inspired by a snail shell, was probably copied from Chantilly chamberpots which predate the Vincennes shape. The factory inventory of 1752 records sixteen *'pots de Chambre forme de Limasson fleurs filet d'or'* ('chamberpots, snail shape with flowers and gold border') valued at twelve *livres* each but described as *médiocres*.[1]

The exceptionally well-painted flowers are likely to have been copied from engravings. A few flowers on early Vincennes porcelains have been traced to M.S. Mérian, *L'Histoire dés Insectes d'Europe*, (Amsterdam, 1730).[1]

Bibliography: Eriksen and Bellaigue, 1987, p. 217

Mark: interlaced *LL*s enclosing a dot painted over the glaze in blue
H. 10 cm., max. l. 22 cm.
Bequeathed by Sir Bernard Eckstein Bt., 1948.158.11
Comparable examples: Musée national de Céramique, Sèvres, illus. Préaud and d'Albis, 1991, p. 147, no. 104

[1] T. Préaud, 'Recherches sur les sources iconographiques utilisées par les décorateurs de porcelaines de Vincennes (1740–1756)', *Bulletin de la Société de l'Histoire de l'Art français,* 1990, pp. 105–15

Painted mark

43 Pair of plates *(assiettes à cordonnet)*
Vincennes, about 1752–3

Moulded, heavily potted. The shape, called *assiette à cordonnet* at the factory on account of the moulded design imitating cord or braid, here picked out in gold, was probably designed by Jean-Claude Duplessis, royal goldsmith from 1758. It seems only to have been used during 1752, when many plate shapes were coming into production. It was sold with landscape, fruit[1] or bird decoration as well as puce-coloured *enfants camayeux* (children painted in one colour). The child fishing is based on an engraving entitled *Pescheurs* from a series published by Huquier of *Jeux d'Enfants* (childrens' games) by François Boucher. The goat appears in the same series in a print called *Fête de Baccus (sic)* and the putto underneath it is probably adapted from *Le Retour de Chasse*.[2]

The hole in each footrim shows that the plates were hung in the glaze kiln on pointed metal supports to separate them and prevent sticking. These devices were first used in 1752.[3] The lack of any date-letter indicates that the plates were completed before 1753.

Drawings by François Boucher (1703–70) and engravings after his work were especially influential at Vincennes and Sèvres[4] (see no. *45*) and were also used as sources at other French porcelain factories, such as Chantilly.[5]

Marks: interlaced *LLs* and dots painted over the glaze in blue; incised *W* (1971.331)
D. 24.5 cm.
Bequeathed by W.R.B. Young 1971.331 and 332
Comparable examples: Louvre Museum, Paris, illus, Préaud and d'Albis, 1991, p. 154, no. 122

[1] Ashmolean Museum WA 1974.264
[2] P. Jean-Richard, *L'oeuvre gravé de François Boucher dans la Collection Edmond de Rothschild*, Paris 1978, nos 226, 228, 227; *Porcelaines de Vincennes*, 1977–1978, no. 11; cf. Malgras (ed.), 1983, p. 188
[3] A. d'Albis, 'Procédés de fabrication de la porcelaine tendre de Vincennes, d'après les livres de Hellot', *Faenza*, vol. LXIX, 1983, pp. 202–215
[4] See R. Savill, 'François Boucher and the Porcelains of Vincennes and Sèvres', *Apollo*, vol. 115 (1982), no. 241, pp. 162–170
[5] Victoria and Albert Museum, London, inv. nos. C. 1297 and 1298–1901

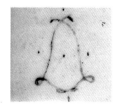

Painted mark

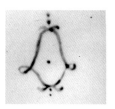

Painted mark

61

44 Pair of glass-coolers *(seaux à verre forme du Roy)*
Vincennes, 1753

Moulded with four panels and fluted in slight relief near rim, thickly potted, the handles moulded with husks and with elaborate terminals.

A drawing survives at the factory for the form, devised by J.-C. Duplessis. It was in production by October 1752 when examples painted with flowers and embellished with a gold line *(fleurs filet d'or)* were listed in the factory inventory. As it is sometimes called *seau du Roy à liqueur* in the factory records, the cooler may have had an alternative use for chilling liqueur-bottles.

The violet ground colour, prepared with a flux of yellow and blue glass and fulminating gold[1] is excessively rare. It is known only on two large *pots-pourris Pompadour* once in the Rosebery Collection at Mentmore and now in the Sèvres Museum,[2] on a tankard and cover[3] and on a pair of vases in a private collection.[4]

The mark of a cross and dot on these coolers is similar to the one attributed to Philippe Xhrowet, best known as a flower painter at Vincennes/Sèvres.[5]

These coolers are probably the pair sold to an unnamed buyer on 21 August 1753 at 72 *livres* each.

Bibliography: S. Eriksen, 'Rare pieces of Vincennes and Sèvres porcelain and a new source for the study of the Manufacture Royale', *Apollo*, LXXXVII, 1968, pp. 34–39, fig. 1; Eriksen and Bellaigue, 1987, p. 263, no. 78; Préaud and d'Albis, 1991, p. 127, no. 53

Marks: Interlaced *LLs* enclosing a dot; painter's mark of a cross above a dot near the footrim painted in blue enamel; *i* incised on 1948.158.5.1 and 2; similar marks on the other cooler with the addition of *H* incised
H. 12.5 cm.
Slight damage to foot
Bequeathed by Sir Bernard Eckstein Bt., 1948
Bensimon Collection

[1] For the development of colours at Vincennes see Préaud and d'Albis, 1991, esp. p. 206
[2] Mentmore sale, Sotheby's, 24 May 1977, Lot 2009; Brunet and Préaud, 1978, no. 52
[3] Sotheby's, 21 November 1978, lot 132, illus. Préaud and d'Albis, 1991, p. 127, No. 51
[4] Préaud and d'Albis, 1991, p. 127, no. 54
[5] Rosalind Savill (in corresp. with writer, 1995) suggests it may be Binet's mark; see Savill, 1988, vol. III, p. 1002 for Binet, pp. 1077–8 for Xhrowet

Painted mark

Incised mark

45   Cup and saucer (gobelet Hébert et soucoupe)
Vincennes, 1753

Moulded, applied twisted handle. Painted over the glaze in the palette known at the Vincennes factory as *camaïeu bleu* (one-colour blue) with children in landscapes after Boucher, probably by the painter André-Charles Vieillard who specialised in this type of decoration. The yellow ground, once much favoured by collectors and in consequence much faked, was first produced at Vincennes around 1751.[1] The date-letter *A* which appears within the factory mark of interlaced *LLs* standing for King Louis XV on the base of both pieces was introduced during 1753. It seems likely that it was not in use from January, however, as there are some discrepancies between the date-letters and the dates of pieces traceable in the surviving factory records.

Cups and saucers of this form were first made in 1752. A smaller second and third size were in production in 1753 and 1754 respectively. By 1754 the cups were being matched with a sugar bowl and cover and an oval lobed stand and were intended for tea.[2]

In the Ashmolean Museum is another yellow-ground cup and saucer of the form known as *Calabre* painted with children in flesh tones with the same painter's mark.[3]

H. of cup. 6.6 cm.; d. of saucer 14 cm.
Marks: date-letter *A* enclosed by interlaced *LLs* with three dots above and one below; cup incised *C*
Bequeathed by Sir Bernard Eckstein Bt., 1948.158.7 1 & 2
Comparable examples: Ader Tajan, Hôtel George V, Paris, 18 November 1992, Lot 19

[1] Préaud and d'Albis, 1991, no. 42, three cups and saucers with yellow ground mentioned in Orry de Fulvy's inventory, May 1751
[2] *Ibid.*, 1991, no. 186, p. 176, col. ill. p. 78
[3] WA 1948.158.8. 1 & 2

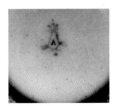

Painted mark

64

46   Chamberpot *(Pot de chambre rond)* in gilt metal mount
Vincennes, 1753

Thrown, rim gilt, gilt band near foot. Below the gilt bronze mount at one side can be seen the two 'scars' where the handle was once attached, which have been painted over. The pot was presumably mounted in ormolu because it had been damaged, but exactly when this occurred is uncertain, as it is notoriously difficult to date ormolu unless it bears the crowned *C* stamp used between 1745–9 when a tax was levied on gilt-bronze.[1]

Chamberpots, first made in French porcelain at Chantilly in the 1730s, were in production at Vincennes by early January 1750, when two were purchased for the Dauphine from the Paris merchant Lazare Duvaux for the substantial sum of 48 *livres*. They were made in several sizes and shapes and with a wide variety of decors over a long period and were still for sale throughout the nineteenth century. A 'new model', presumably corresponding to this example, was introduced in 1752.[2] For yellow as a ground colour, see *45*.

This piece is reputed to have belonged to the controller of finances M. de Machault (1701–94), forebear of the writer and collector the comte de Chavagnac (see below). The Sèvres factory records show that Machault purchased a chamberpot with a yellow ground and coloured flowers on 8 August 1753 for 48 *livres*.[3]

Marks: interlaced *LL*s and the mark of the painter Vincent Taillandier painted over the glaze in blue; incised *C, O* or *G*
H. 14.6 cm.; max. l. (incl. mounts) 20.7 cm.
Bequeathed by Sir Bernard Eckstein Bt., 1948.158.1; comte de Chavagnac collection (part of his collection label adheres to the base), Paris, Drouot, 19–21 June 1911, Lot 256, described as *'Jardinière de forme ronde, en ancienne porcelaine tendre de Vincennes... Décor de Taillandier Ancienne collection de Machault'*

[1] P. Verlet, *Les Bronzes Dorés français du XVIIIe siècle*, n.p., 1987, pp. 268–71
[2] Cf. Préaud and d'Albis, 1991, p. 161, no. 142
[3] MNS, Archives de Sèvres, Vy 1, f. 15

Painted mark

Incised mark

47 Cooler for a half-bottle *(seau à demi-bouteille)*
Sèvres, 1757

Moulded, the shape was devised at Vincennes around 1752 and copied quite closely at Chantilly.[1]

The richly tooled gilt pattern around the reserves includes trellis and diaper designs typical of early production at Sèvres, and not dissimilar to the gilding on two orange tubs in the British Museum also painted with flowers and fruit on a green ground.[2] One is dated 1756 and was decorated by the same (unidentified) painter, perhaps Jean-Pierre Boulanger.[3]

The Meissen factory in Saxony, whose porcelain Vincennes aimed to rival, developed ground colours in the 1730s. By 1747 the formula for green using copper oxide was known at Vincennes, as the notebooks of its chemist, Jean Hellot, demonstrate. The mordant for preparing the surface for ground colour was unknown there until 1751. Green grounds came into production in 1753. Initially of the pale almost turquoise hue seen on this piece, it was sometimes uneven in appearance, perhaps because only one layer of colour was used.

Marks: date-letter *E* enclosed by interlaced *LL*s above *B* perhaps for the painter Jean-Pierre Boulanger in blue enamel; incised *J* for an unknown workman
H. 13.5 cm.; d. not incl. handles 13.8 cm.
Purchased, 1979.95

[1] See Malgras (ed.), 1983, p. 54, 58, 60 (two sizes), 66, dating from c.1750–70. The Vincennes form is discussed in Préaud and d'Albis, 1991, see p. 154
[2] Dawson, 1994, no. 83, 84
[3] For his career see Savill, 1988, III, p. 1005

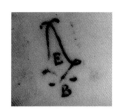

Painted mark

48   Plate *(assiette à palmes)* from a service made
      for Marie-Caroline of Naples and the two
      Sicilies
      Sèvres, 1773

Moulded, the painted monogram *CL* of flowers below a
wreath stands for Queen (Marie) Caroline of Naples
(also called Charlotte-Louise) and her daughter Louise,
born on 27 July 1773. Married to Ferdinand, later,
Ferdinand IV of Naples and III of Sicily in 1768, Caroline
was Empress Maria Theresa's daughter and sister of
Marie-Antoinette, Queen of France. In later life she took
a leading part in the affairs of her adopted country.
        King Louis XV was the godfather of Caroline's
child. The service which he presented to the Queen con-
sisted of six place settings and was delivered on 4
December 1773. Its total cost, including the biscuit
sculpture for table decoration, amounted to 12,424 *livres*.

[1] Savill, 1988, Vol. III,
pp. 1073–4
[2] I am grateful to
Rosalind Savill for
this suggestion

D. 24.8 cm.
Purchased, 1972.125
Marks: interlaced *LL*s enclosing date-letter *U* for 1773 above *W* for
the painter François Vavasseur or one of his family[1] and with *Z* at
the right perhaps for the painter Joyau[2] painted in blue enamel; hole
for suspension in footrim

49   Tureen, cover and stand *(pot à oglio)*,
glass-cooler *(seau à verre)* and monteith
or glass-cooler *(seau crenelé)* from a service
for Marie-Antoinette
Sèvres, 1784

Moulded crenellated cooler of hard-paste porcelain.
There are two identically-decorated services, one
ordered by Marie-Antoinette in January 1784 for the
Tuileries Palace and a second (in fact the one originally
envisioned for the Queen) presented by her husband to
Gustav III of Sweden, when he visited France in June
1784. In August 1784 the Queen's service was delivered
to her.

Both services comprised over 300 pieces.[1] The
tureen was one of two placed at either side of the table
for serving *oglio* or *oille*, a meat and vegetable stew.[2]
The shape, was made at Vincennes from around
1752–53.[3] The companion tureen, cover and stand is in
the State Hermitage Museum, St. Petersburg.[4]

Both wine-glass coolers belonged to the second
(dessert) service. The crenellated cooler was known in
the eighteenth century as a 'monteith'.[5] Glasses rested
bowl downwards on ice, their stems supported on the
crenellations.

For glass coolers of the simpler form see *41*.

The service was copied in the nineteenth century
at the Herend factory in Hungary.[6]

A service, recorded as 'Service No. B', delivered
to the comtesse d'Artois in June 1789 was slightly less
expensive, but is so similar to this service that the two
have often been confused.

H. of tureen and cover. 26.1 cm.; l. of stand 46.3 cm. Tureen cracked
Marks: Interlaced *LL*s enclosing date-letters *GG* for 1784, mark of
the painter La Roche, above *LG* in gold for the gilder Le Guay; stand
incised *25a* and *A/14*
Given anonymously in memory of Sir Bruce and Lady Richmond,
1974.329.1 and 2; Sir E. Radcliffe Collection, Christie's, 29 October
1973, Lot 154

H. of wine-glass cooler 10.6 cm.
Marks: Interlaced *LL*s enclosing date-letters *GG* for 1784 below *g.*
for the painter C.-N. Buteux[7] and above *LF* for the gilder A.J. Foinet,
called La France,[8] incised *17* and *48a*
Provenance: as above, Lot 156 (one of four) (1974.332)

H. without handles of crenellated glass-cooler 13.3 cm.; l. without
handles: 25.5 cm.
Marks: Interlaced *LL*s enclosing date-letters *GG* for 1784 below a
crown and above *bq* for the painter Bauquerre, *HP* for the painter
Henry Prévost all in gold; hole for suspension
Provenance: as above, Lot 155, plate 24 (one of two) (1974.331)

[1] Forty-seven pieces sold
at Drouot-Richelieu,
Paris, 15 December
1993, Lot 108 A-T Lots
165, 166, 167, 168; for
pieces at Versailles see
C. Baulez, 'Versailles
vers un retour de
Sèvres', *Revue du
Louvre*, December
1991, pp. 62–76, and
exh. cat. *Versailles
et les Tables Royales
en Europe XVIIème
– XIXème Siècles*,
November 1993–
February 1994, nos
108, 109
[2] H. Coutts, 'Formal
Dining in Europe',
Antiques, August 1994,
pp. 186–197 and
'The Dinner Service',
*Antique Dealer and
Collectors' Guide*. July
1994, pp 28–31
[3] Préaud and d'Albis,
Paris, 1991, no. 150
[4] Getty Photograph,
Center archive, Santa
Monica, California
[5] Called after a
"fantastical Scot called
'Monsieur Montiegh'",
who wore the bottom
of his cloak or coat
notched at the end
of the seventeenth
century. The word
originates in the
English language
in the 1680s
[6] A Herend plate
in the British Museum
with this pattern is
smaller than any
made by Sèvres in the
eighteenth century;
see Sir A. W. Franks,
*Catalogue of a
Collection of
Continental Porcelain*,
London, 1896, no. 260,
d. 73/4 ins
[7] For Buteux, see Savill,
1988, III, pp. 1009–1010
[8] For La France, see
ibid., p. 1039

Painted mark

Incised mark

Incised mark

Painted mark

Incised mark

Incised mark

Painted mark

71

73

50   Figure of Blaise Pascal (1623–62)
Sèvres, about 1784

Hard-paste biscuit (unglazed) porcelain, moulded. In front of the philosopher and mathematician, shown in clerical dress, is an open book inscribed *Lettres à un provincial* (1656). His left hand cradles a tablet incised with a diagram of a cycloid, probably referring to his experiments on the measurement of air.

In 1780 King Louis XVI commissioned the series of *Grands Hommes de France*[1] from Sèvres. These porcelain reductions of the marble statues in the Louvre were based on terracottas[2] made at the King's command by the sculptors of the marbles, in this case by Augustin Pajou (1730–1809).[3] The reductions were shown at the 1783 *Salon*. Although the figures, intended for the King's library at Versailles, and originally sold from Sèvres at 360 *livres*, were never a commercial success, they remained in production up to the beginning of this century, and are impressive works of sculpture in their own right.

Bibliography: N. Penny, 'A Statuette of Pascal for the Ashmolean Museum', *NACF Review*, 1986 pp. 128-9; N. Penny, *Catalogue of European Sculpture in the Ashmolean Museum 1540 to the Present Day*, Oxford, 1992, Vol. II, no. 293

Mark: *M* or *W* incised for an unknown workman, *1*
H. 31.8 cm.; d. 29 cm.
Purchased through the MGC/V&A Fund, the National Art Collections Fund and the Friends of the Ashmolean (WA 1985.191); apparently originally bought by Gouverneur Morris, the American Minister to France during the Revolution, from the Tuileries Palace and presented by him to Mrs Anthony Walton-White, sold Christie's, 25 March 1985, Lot 27
Inkwell and quill missing, small chips to scroll

[1] See S. Taylor, 'Artists and *Philosophes* as mirrored by Sèvres and Wedgwood', in *The Artist and Writer in France, Essays in Honour of Jean Seznec*, ed. F. Haskell, A. Levi, R. Shackleton, Oxford, 1974, pp. 21-39; A. McClellan, 'La série des 'Grands Hommes' de la France du comte d'Angiviller et la politique des Parlements', in *Clodion et la sculpture française de la fin du XVIIIe siècle*, proc. colloq., Louvre, Paris, 1992, pp. 223-249; for Descartes see Louvre, *Nouvelles acquisitions du département des Objets d'art 1990–1994*, Paris, 1995, no. 87
[2] The model in the Musée national de Céramique, Sèvres, is illus. by J. Gaborit, *Diderot et l'art de Boucher*, exh. Paris, Hôtel de la Monnaie, 1984–5, pp 474–6, no. 142
[3] Pajou was a pupil of J.-B Lemoyne; in Rome from 1752–6, he became a member of the Academy in 1760 and its Rector in 1792. He specialised in portraits

75

51 Figure of a pregnant woman holding a bundle

Possibly Orleans factory, about 1760–70

Soft-paste porcelain, moulded, lead glazed, rather thin concave base partly splashed with glaze underneath. She wears a wide-brimmed hat with a shallow crown perched on the left side of her head which is turned slightly to right. Her dress has a low square neck and sleeves to the elbows with cuffs. Her left hand rests on her protruding stomach and her right holds an unidentified object, the front part of which is snapped off. The details of the strap and buckle on her high-heeled shoes are carefully incised.

Black specks, several 'tears' or holes in the paste, and pooling of the greenish glaze around her feet show that the factory was experiencing technical problems.

No other example of this figure is known, and it is an unusually realistic depiction of a woman. For once the subject is not a dancer or a vendor and wears an ordinary rather nondescript costume rather than fashionable attire. Once attributed to the Mennecy factory, its static attitude perhaps betrays its origin in one of the lesser-known soft-paste factories such as that at Orleans.

Bibliography: Dawson, 1993, p. 16, fig. 4

Unmarked
H. 21.4 cm.
Given by Cyril Andrade, 1968.249; sold Sotheby's, 9 March 1965, Lot 80
Comparable examples: René Fribourg Collection: V French Faience and European Porcelain Part 2, Sotheby's, 15 October 1963, Lot 407 to Lacroix, £140

52   Pair of figures of seated harvesters
Factory uncertain, perhaps about 1765–70

Soft-paste porcelain, rather greyish, tin glazed, moulded, flat base splashed with glaze. The woman holds a sickle in her right hand. At her left is a container, its upper edge glazed, perhaps intended as a vase. In the left pocket of her companion's long jacket, which covers his shirt, is a bottle. A (?) bread roll pokes out from a hole in the pocket. His right hand holds a branch springing from the tree stump on which he is sitting. In his left hand he clutches an unidentified small object pierced by a small circular hole. At his right side, resting on the grassy mound which supports him, is a container, its upper edge glazed, perhaps intended as a vase.

Both figures have several holes of irregular shape at the back and front and it is not clear whether these are intentional and if so what their purpose might be. It is likely that they are defects in the manufacturing process attributable to the lack of plasticity of the clay making it difficult to model.

These figures seem unrelated in size and general appearance to those made at the Chantilly factory. The faces, in particular, are rather too coarse, and the quality of the workmanship differs from other more accomplished Chantilly pieces. It is possible that they were made at one of the lesser-known soft-paste factories, but exactly which of these is still an open question.

For a similar white glazed seated male figure in a hat with a sword in his left hand and a bag in his right see below.[1]

Unmarked
H. of woman 24.8 cm.; h. of man 23.8 cm.
Given by Cyril Andrade, 1972.351; sold Sotheby's, 5 December 1972, Lot 129

[1] Reproduced courtesy the Board of Trustees of the Victoria and Albert Museum. Museum no. C.345-1909

Works referred to in the text

B. Beaucamp-Markowsky, *Boîtes en Porcelaine des manufactures européennes au 18e siècle*, Fribourg, 1985

H. Coutts, 'The Sign of the Hunting Horn', *Antique Collector*, Vol. 69, no. 9, October 1991, pp. 80–83

A. Dawson, 'From Pleasure to Propaganda: French 18th Century Porcelain Figures, Groups, Plaques and Medallions', *Handbook*, The International Fine Art and Antique Dealers' show, 7th Regiment Armory, Park Avenue at 67th Street, New York City, 15–21 October 1993, pp. 13-19

A. Dawson, *A Catalogue of French Porcelain in the British Museum*, London, 1994

P. Dupont, *Porcelaines françaises aux XVIIIe et XIXe siècles*, Paris, 1987

S. Eriksen, *The David Collection*, Copenhagen, 1980

S. Eriksen and G. de Bellaigue, *Sèvres Porcelain, Vincennes and Sèvres 1740–1800*, London, 1987

C. Frégnac (ed.), *Les porcelainiers du XVIIIe siècle français*, Paris, 1964

R. de Plinval de Guillebon, *Musée du Louvre, département des Objets d'art, Catalogue des porcelaines françaises*, Paris, 1992

R. de Plinval de Guillebon, 'Les céramistes du Faubourg Saint-Antoine avant 1750', *Bull. de la Soc. de l'hist. de Paris et de l'Ile de France*, 117ème année, 1990, Paris, 1992, pp. 159-218

R. de Plinval de Guillebon, *Faïence et Porcelaine de Paris XVIII–XIXe siècles*, Dijon, 1995

G.-J. Malgras (ed.), *Porcelaines tendres françaises*, Paris, 1983

T. Préaud and A. d'Albis, *La porcelaine de Vincennes*, Paris, 1991

G. Savage, *Seventeenth and Eighteenth Century French Porcelain*, London, 1960

R. Savill, *The Wallace Collection, Catalogue of Sèvres Porcelain*, London, 1988, 3 vols

R. Savill, 'A Sèvres treasure house at Waddesdon, Re-assembling the Starhemberg service', *Apollo*, CXXXIX, 386, April 1994, pp. 25-33

Exhibitions

Meissener Porzellan: R. Rückert, *Meissener Porzellan 1710–1810*, Bayerisches Nationalmuseum, Munich, 1966

Porcelaines de Vincennes: A. Hallé and T. Préaud, *Porcelaines de Vincennes, les Origines de Sèvres*, Grand Palais, Paris, 1977-78

Isaacson Collection: Armin B. Allen, *The Henry C. and Martha L. Isaacson Collection*, London, June 1987 (catalogue of a selling exhibition)

Porcelain for Palaces: J. Ayers, O. Impey, J. Mallet, *Porcelain for Palaces: the Fashion for Japan in Europe 1650–1750*, British Museum, London, 1990